# Dynamic Dialog

A Quick Guide to Writing Well

P.S. Wells

Pegwood Publishing

Title: Dynamic Dialog

By P.S. Wells

Subjects: 1. Authorship Reference (Books)

2. Writing Skill Reference (Books)

3. Creativity (Books)

Key Words: How to write, plot, creativity, fiction writing, write story, write fiction

ISBN ebook: 979-8-9921044-2-4

ISBN paperback: 979-8-9921044-3-1

Published by Pegwood Publishing

Roanoke IN 46783

# Contents

# Chapter One

---

# On Your Mark, Get Set, Write

B efore you begin writing, save time and effort by knowing these three things.

1. What is your idea?

2. Who is your audience?

3. How does your idea, message, or story benefit your audience?

4. What is the best method to share your idea to your particular audience?

Every project begins with an idea.

**First**, decide what is the story or message, lesson or insight you want to share?

Hone the idea down to a laser point. The tighter the focus the better you stay on target. The tighter the message the easier for your reader to follow where you take them.

Do not be intimidated to find others have written on the same topic. You have your own slant, your own experience, your own insight which is unique to you. There is always room in the market for fresh ways of thinking on a familiar topic. Your voice will be different from other authors.

Put considerable thought into how you will present your idea in a unique fashion.

What is your idea?

**Second**, you have an idea, message, or story you want to share. The question is, who do you want to share your message with?

Before you begin, clarify exactly who you are speaking to. This is as important as dialing a specific number when you make a phone call.

No project—outside God's Word—is for everyone. Who is your target audience? Who is interested in receiving your message?

Age, education level, ethnicity, faith, gender, hobbies, interests, and profession are among the considerations when you define your audience. Academics, artists, and athletes each have unique jargon and terminology as do zoning specialists, zoologists, and zoo keepers. Bestselling author, Jerry Jenkins, pictured his mother sitting across the desk as he wrote his novels. She represented the audience he had in mind for the stories he told.

How specific can you be when you describe your audience?

- *The Ten Best Decisions A Single Mom Can Make* is practical help and tangible tips for solo parents ages 24 to 45, eager to create a healthy and successful family.

- *Slavery in the Land of the Free* informs intermediate and high school students about human trafficking in the United States.

- Geared for four to eight-year-olds, *The Girl Who Wore Freedom* is the true story of five-year-old Dany who was given Lifesavers and liberty on D-Day.

Writing to children is completely different from communicating with teens which differs from sharing with adults. Generally speaking, the vocabulary that appeals to women is not the same as the descriptions that resonate with men. While the words in a toddler's board book are chosen as carefully as the text for a novel, the volume is exceedingly less. Knowing your audience guides your vocabulary level and the length of your project in the same way you craft a conversation with an industry professional far differently than you prepare to talk with a child.

**Third**, how does your idea, message, or story benefit your audience? Why would your reader trade their hard-earned funds to purchase your project? Why would someone invest their limited time to read your writing?

In other words, what take-home value do you provide?

Types of take-home value writers offer include

- entertainment

- education

- guidance

- humor

- how-to instruction

- inspiration

- information

When you pen a project to be viewed and consumed by others, you create an exchange. You expect your audience to read your writing. Your audience expects you will make the experience of reading your work worthwhile. To keep your end of the agreement, clarify the benefit you plan to provide. Purposefully and generously give your audience abundant take-home value.

**Fourth**, once you know your audience and the take-home value you will provide to that audience, it's time to decide on the best vehicle to convey your message. There are myriad ways for a writer to communicate including

apps
articles

books
children's books
curriculum
greeting cards
novel
screenplay
song
web content

As writers, we have myriad formats to connect with readers. When you know your target audience and the take-home value you want to deliver, then consider what format will be the most effective to share your message. You have plenty of options.

A writer has one job to do and that is to elicit an emotional response in the reader. When you write a book or want to improve a story, dialog is often the heart of the story. How can you use dialog to elicit emotion within your reader?

# Chapter Two

# Dialog Is

You have a story to share, a message to tell through writing. There are foundational aspects to writing well including a well-crafted plot.

Essentials for a powerful story are

1. a character the reader cares about

2. a very great life-changing, world-impacting need the character must achieve

3. a great obstacle between the character we care about and the character's life-changing, world-impacting need

Critical elements for a compelling, memorable story that works include

- Pivotal Plots

- Memorable Characters

- Sensational Settings

- Dynamic Dialog

- Point of View

Dialogue or Dialog?

Dialogue is a conversation between two or more.

Primarily found in North America, dialog is an alternative spelling of the word dialogue. This alternative spelling became popular in the 1980s as a computer term and morphed into the spelling used most often in the United States. The Oxford English Dictionary still shows the preferred spelling as dialogue.

Beyond the spelling question,

Dialog is what characters say. Powerful stories are dialog-driven through carefully chosen word selections. The four purposes of dialog in your story include:

1. Move your story forward
2. Reveal something important about your plot
3. Show something important about your character
4. Give your character a unique voice

In Luke 1:30-33 Scripture reports, "The angel said to her, "Do not be afraid, Mary; you have found favor with God. You will conceive and give birth to a son, and you are to call him Jesus. He will be great and will be called the Son of the Most High. The Lord God will give him the throne of his father David, and he will reign over Jacob's descendants forever; his kingdom will never end."

With a relatively short conversation, the angel provides a lot of information that greatly moves forward the story of God's plan for the world.

2. Reveal something important about your plot.

The angel of the Lord provides a vital and life-changing plot point when the angel says to the shepherds, "Do not be afraid. I bring you good news that will cause great joy for all the people. Today in the town of David a Savior has been born to you; he is the Messiah, the Lord. This will be a sign to you: You will find a baby wrapped in cloths and lying in a manger," (Luke 2:10-12).

3. Show something important about your character.

After Jesus was born in Bethlehem in Judea, during the time of King Herod, Magi from the east came to Jerusalem and asked, "Where is the one who has been born king of the Jews? We saw his star when it rose and have come to worship him," (Matthew 2:1-3).

Scripture says Herod was greatly disturbed by the report of the Wisemen. Herod sent the wise men to Bethlehem with these instructions, "Go and search carefully for the child. As soon as you find him, report to me, so that I too may go and worship him."

With this concise exchange, we quickly understand the integrity of the wise men who traveled long and far to worship the Savior. We also see the cunning and conniving character of Herod.

4. Give your character a unique voice.

When Simeon takes the eight-day-old Christ child into his arms, we hear the unique voice of a faithful saint who has waited on the Lord's timing and understands his own place in the story.

Simeon praised God, saying: "Sovereign Lord, as you have promised, you may now dismiss your servant in peace. For my eyes have seen your salvation, which you have prepared in the sight of all nations: a light for revelation to the Gentiles, and the glory of your people Israel," (Luke 2:28-32).

When writing, filter your dialog through these four purposes to be certain the segment is earning its place as a contributor to your project.

If the words your characters are speaking do not add to your story, how can you reword or add value to your dialog? After all, the conversations that take place between characters are often the reader's favorite part.

# Chapter Three

## Dialog Worth Quoting

L ike delicious desserts, dialog is often a reader's favorite part of a story. We quote great dialog for generations.

"Off with her head!" – Lewis Carroll.

"We make a living by what we get, we make a life by what we give." – Winston Churchill.

"There's so much scope for imagination." – Lucy Maud Montgomery.

"It's me again, Hank the Cowdog." – John Erickson.

"It is only with the heart that one can see rightly; what is essential is invisible to the eye." – Antoine de Saint-Exupéry.

"Give back to Caesar what is Caesar's and to God what is God's." – Jesus Christ.

My family has admitted that if film and book quotes were removed, our vocabulary would be reduced by half. How about you? Do you quote dialog? How many of these can you place?

Go ahead, make my day.
All that is gold does not glitter, Not all those who wander are lost.
Whatever our souls are made of, his and mine are the same.
Wish I could say yes, but I can't.
This above all: To thine own self be true.
Stupid is as stupid does.
I'm gonna make him an offer he can't refuse.
Anything worth dying for is certainly worth living for.
God bless us, everyone.
You should be kissed and often, and by someone who knows how.
You're braver than you believe, stronger than you seem, and smarter than you think.

Love is patient. Love is kind. It does not envy. It does not boast, it is not proud. It is not rude, it is not self-seeking, it is not easily angered. It keeps no record of wrongs. Love does not delight in evil but rejoices with the truth. It always protects, always trusts, always hopes, always perseveres.

The one thing that doesn't abide by majority rule is a person's conscience.

We're not in Kansas anymore.
Snap out of it.

Sometimes, I've believed as many as six impossible things before breakfast.

Houston, we have a problem.

Show me the money.

I feel the need, the need for speed.

There is no try, only do.

Is the sun up? Put it on your left.

You complete me.

Get your stinking paws off me, you dirty ape.

Wax on, wax off.

Shaken, not stirred.

I can do this all day.

Hasta la vista, Baby.

You're gonna need a bigger boat.

Do I love you? My god, if your love were a grain of sand, mine would be a universe of beaches.

Just keep swimming.

My precious.

You is kind, you is smart, you is important.

You had me at hello.

Help me, Obi Won Kenobi, you're my only hope.

I wish I had done everything with you.

To infinity and beyond.

You must allow me to tell you how ardently I admire and love you.

Every time a bell rings, an angel gets his wings.

Of all the gin joints in the world, she walks into mine.

No touchy.

All we have to decide is what to do with the time that is given us.

There's no place like home.

You can be my wingman any day.

As writers, how do we craft words into dialog that outlives our writing? What are the common ingredients that make a piece of dialog live beyond the story? We will talk about the making of dynamic dialog next.

In the meantime, what dialog from a book or film do you quote?

## Chapter Four

# How To Keep Dialog Fresh

There is an art to writing dialog that takes place between multiple characters, yet the topic remains the same. Different conversations, same subject matter. How can you discuss a person, incident, or event multiple times without repeating facts?

Once your reader already knows something, resist being tedious by repeating that same information. When another character must be informed of the news already revealed, share the information in a way that

- does not repeat what the reader knows

- does give the reader new information

For instance, in *Chasing Sunrise* the reader knows from a previous chapter that Michael has been on an assignment that went sideways. To keep from boring the reader into a coma, and to increase suspense, each time this incident is spoken about, characters must talk about it with fresh information.

Here is the first excerpt on the topic:

Michael barged into his commanding officer's office. Corbin waved him to a chair, but Michael walked straight to the large desk and tossed his parajumper insignia across the dark wood surface. "You used me."

Corbin calmly regarded Michael. "I heard there was an incident on your last assignment."

"I didn't become one of America's fighting elite to kill women."

"My information was sketchy, Michael. We were ordered to protect the patient."

Michael waved a hand at the television on a low coffee table. Though presently muted, the screen showed Bennett Taylor wiping his eye. "The patient was a general's wife who was mysteriously hospitalized."

"Don't you watch the news? Taylor's a senator now." Corbin crossed the room and closed the office door. "A general's wife or a senator's wife should receive extra protection."

"Mr. God-and-Country barred all visitors and ordered life support withheld. That's not protection. It's a death sentence."

Corbin returned to his desk. "But you did apprehend someone who was making an attempt on the patient."

"I apprehended her father, Corbin. Her father was attempting to give water to his only child."

Corbin indicated the chair again. "Sit down, Northington."

"No."

"I'll look into things, Michael."

"Don't bother. She died."

"Take some time off." Corbin picked up the insignia and held it out for Michael. "Cool down." The metal flash in Corbin's hand was the image of an angel enfolding the world in its wings.

"I'm done." Michael turned and walked away. He had his hand on the doorknob when Corbin spoke again.

"Did you know her?"

Michael stopped, pausing before he answered. "Yeah, I knew her."

Of course, there also has to be a conversation about what is going to happen next with Michael's partner. How can the writer provide fresh insights about the same topic to the person closest to our protagonist and the one who was there when it all happened?

Second excerpt:

Bryce casually slung an arm across the back of his chair and looked pointedly toward the discarded want ads. "So, battle buddy, what's the plan?"

"I'm making this up as I go."

"This from the guy who was on a fast track to his goals when he was still in diapers." Bryce signaled the waitress and turned his attention back to Michael. "You were prepubescent when you joined the Civil Air Patrol."

"I was fourteen and you weren't."

"Being the older, more mature member of this dynamic duo, I was sixteen." Bryce folded his sunglasses into his shirt pocket. "And driving myself to meetings while your mom dropped you off in that stylish station wagon."

Remembering, Michael smirked. "You were driving that rust-fringed, dilapidated pick-up truck older than Methuselah."

"Don't poke fun at that ride, Mikey," Bryce warned. "It got us to a lot of great places."

"Training weekends, ground team practice, survival school, flight school..."

"You made it through the toughest training regimen in the world." Bryce leaned forward on the table. "Parajumper is all you've wanted to be since you were sixteen. It's what you've been for ten years."

Studying his mug, Michael nodded.

"Come back, partner."

Michael spun his glass in slow circles, the condensation leaving wet rings on the table. "I can't."

Bryce sighed. "This is about the general's wife."

"What's our prime directive, Bryce?"

"So that others may live."

"Two people have done something for me in my life." Michael met his gaze. "One of them was Verity. They used me to kill her. I can't work for people like that."

When writing dialog, avoid repeating facts the reader already knows. Instead, consider how you can believably drip fresh information for the reader into each conversation.

18

# Chapter Five

---

# What To Leave Out Of Dialog

Whan people speak to one another, we often say one thing while meaning something completely different. In other words, we are adept at not meaning what we say, and not saying what we mean.

When possible, duplicate this situation in writing your dialog. In this segment of a conversation between a teenager and his mother from *Chasing Sunrise,* the spoken words are different from what is truly being communicated. Yet both understand the underlying topic.

Excerpt:

The second week, the commander handed Michael's application form back to him. "Need your dad's signature."

Michael brought home the forms and dropped them on his bedroom dresser. The third week, when his mom hurried everyone through a spaghetti and green bean dinner so they could make the meeting, he finally said he wasn't going.

"Why not?"

"Just not."

"You wanna be in this or not?"

"I can't."

"Why not?"

"Something about the forms."

She picked up his empty plate, stacked it on top of hers, and carried them to the kitchen. "Get them."

It took his mother a nanosecond to see the problem. She picked up an ink pen and boldly signed her name where a father's signature was required. "That should take care of things." She handed him the completed form. "Now let's go."

Similarly, when Michael and his battle buddy have this conversation, while it appears they are talking about the girl they met that evening, a closer look reveals they are really thinking about Michael's sister who he had not been able to protect from harm.

Excerpt:

Outside under the stars Michael could hear strains of the band's attempt to play Elvis' *All Shook Up*. He fished in his pocket and pulled out the money that was there. Reaching for the girl's hand, he pressed the bills into her palm. "Go home," he told her kindly. "Find another job."

She looked from him to the bar. Bryce still filled the doorway, his back to Michael and the girl. Her eyes met Michael's again and he saw the same fear there he had seen in the little bird's.

He indicated the bills in her hand. "Should be enough until you find something better."

She counted the money in her hand. When she looked at him again, there was hope in her eyes where fear had been a moment ago.

"Now go." Michael spoke gently.

She gripped the bills tightly and stuffed them inside the front of her dress. As Bryce stepped backwards out of the doorway, the girl turned and fled.

Standing beside Michael, Bryce stuffed his hands in his pockets. "Mama-san was curious about what was happening with her girl." The two watched the girl disappear into the night.

"And?"

"I gave her some money for her trouble."

Michael grunted and turned toward the hotel. Bryce fell into step beside him. They were nearly back to their hotel when Bryce finally broke the silence. "You okay?"

"She probably wasn't any older than Marissa."

"Probably not."

"She should be playing with dolls."

"Or picking on her older brother's best friend."

Michael smiled, remembering the good-natured pranks his sisters used to do to pester good-natured Bryce. "Remember that first snow when April—"

"Yep."

"And the time you slept over and Marissa—"

"Don't remind me."

They walked on, each lost in his own thoughts. Stopping outside the hotel, Michael asked, "Think she'll do something better with her life?"

Bryce shrugged. "Well, I'd say that's up to her." He slapped Michael on the back. "But you gave her the option."

When possible, layer your dialog with multiple meanings. This can be done with symbolism, hints, word selection, body movement, and references. Trust your reader to be savvy enough to understand and to put the pieces together as the story unfolds.

When can you give your reader several messages at the same time using the same technique we often use in daily dialog with those around us?

# Chapter Six

# When Talking Is Showing, Not Telling

For a writer, dialog is a handy tool to show, instead of tell your reader important information about your character.

The vocabulary of a character lets the reader know if the character is educated, gives clues to the region the character is from, and shows the character's nature to be relaxed, tightly wound, worried, sly, or confident.

Reading this excerpt from *Chasing Sunrise*, the speaker's dialect instantly connects him to his background on the island of St. Croix.

Excerpt:
A nearby local answered Bryce's question. "We go to the crab races, mon."

Bryce and Michael looked over at the eavesdropper, who was keeping pace on his way to somewhere.

"Crab races?" Bryce echoed.

"You're new to the island." With brown eyes and an easy smile, the medium-built man stuck out his hand to Bryce and Michael. "I'm Ned. Native to the island."

At the end of the story, Ned appears in a completely different setting, but he remains the man from the island.

Excerpt:
"Ya' good, mon?" His dark eyes reflected kind reassurance as Brother Ned stressed the accent as he dropped a reassuring hand on Michael's shoulder.

Similarly, readers get to know the character and personality of Corbin McIntyre through the words he uses.

Excerpt:
There was a long silence while Michael and Corbin regarded one another. At last, the CO nodded. "A fair offer is nae cause fur feud." Corbin stood and extended his hand to Michael. "We have an accord."

Corbin's unique vocabulary commonly shows up in his everyday dealings with his team.

Excerpt:
Corbin covered the phone with his hand. "Jings and crivvens, Michael. Shut up and sit down."

Later in the novel, we see Corbin when his temper is up.

Excerpt:
"The Scottish people have a saying, Mr. Northington."
Braced for the verbal onslaught, Michael maintained strict military bearing.
"God takes care of the poor and the stupid." Corbin pushed his face close to Michael's and thrust his finger into Michael's chest, emphasizing every word with a thump against his breastbone. "And you, Mister, are the visual aid for the latter."

Dialog can show a character's personality. Bryce Lassiter, the sidekick in *Chasing Sunrise* is known for remaining calm. Bryce's easy-going personality is reflected in his pattern of droppin' the g at the end of words ending in ing.

Excerpt:
Bryce caught up. "Where we goin,' partner?"

When our hero is at a crossroads, Bryce is the steady presence.
Excerpt:
Bryce took in the scattered newspaper with several items circled in blue ink and Michael's empty glass. "Since I'm the only one here still employed, I'll do the buyin'. What's your brew?"

Bryce lends a casual air even amid tension.

Excerpt:
Bryce peered through the scope. "Somethin's not right."

A conversation tag is another tool to add depth to the personality of a character. In *Riven* by Jerry B. Jenkins, the prison warden commonly answers questions with, "Yanno," a run together of "Yeah, no." Yeah, I heard you and no is the reply.

Introverted Matthew Cuthbert, in the *Anne of Green Gables* feature film answers Anne's many questions with a phrase that gives him a beat to think. "Well, now," he draws out as he collects his thoughts.

Additionally, to keep the story flowing, common filler words are removed from conversations in the editing process. Needless words include

Yeah
Okay
Hello
Good-bye
Oh
Well

The exception is when a filler word is used to spotlight a personality trait such as Matthew Cuthbert's "Well now ..."

In the first draft, dialog may begin with "Hello," "Oh," "Well," or "Yeah," and end with 'Good-bye," but in the editing process, remove these unnecessary distractions that interrupt the flow and pull the reader out of the story.

How can you use dialog to show, instead of tell, your reader vital information about the personality and background of your character?

# Chapter Seven

# What About Profanity?

B y the time she was ten years old, my daughter had surpassed all the art instruction I could give. At a local art show, she considered the pieces on display and pointed to a group of portraits. "I could learn from that artist."

And so she began group lessons at the artist's studio. When I picked her up after the first class, my daughter eagerly described the new techniques she learned and finished with, "And there is a little old lady who swears like crazy."

The following week, the instructor and I talked about my daughter's progress. "She mentioned that one classmate is particularly colorful," I said.

The instructor nodded. "When your daughter joined the class, that student really cleaned up her language."

To use or not to use. What does a writer do with the question of profanity? Writing about our artistic little old lady with the surprising vocabulary, what words get included in the dialog?

When writing about a street gang, an author wants to portray the character authentically. To do anything less will lose readers. When author and filmmaker Frankie Schaeffer produced faith-based films, his biggest challenge was to make a product a church would show while portraying characters realistically. After all, what uncouth leader of a street gang is believably going to say, "Golly gee whillikers"?

Language is a non-issue for some writers, and some publishers have policies that require no profanity. Additionally, including such words limits the audience. Some readers prefer family-friendly works. Projects with mature content are not recommended for younger readers.

So what does a writer do when writing realistically about a character whose language would be populated with profanity? What about those shocking plot points that would illicit such an exclamation even from a character who is not known for using such terms?

When dealing with language choices, here are some work-arounds.

Use a grawlix, the series of keyboard characters that often appear in place of profanity. Think of the symbols as graphically bleeping out unacceptable words. This is often seen in comic books as #@*%.

Use the term that describes for the reader what is said. *The faces of his two sisters filled Michael's mind and he cursed.*

Another term to describe for the reader what is said. *He swore.*

Hint at what is said. *"You son of a..." Marc swung his fist into the man's nose.*

A similar way to hint at what is being said. *"Son of a..." the oath seamlessly streamed into another language that Marc guessed to be Arabic.*

Using profanity just for the sake of using such words is lazy writing, tiresome for the reader, and limits your audience. What other ways can you use to show who the character is while remaining family-friendly? How can you show the seriousness of the situation without the use of profanity?

# Chapter Eight

# Thank You

T hank you for reading *Creative Characters* by P.S. Wells
(PeggySue Wells) in the Quick Guide to Writing Well series
*Creative Characters* is available in ebook and paperback.

If you have a moment, please leave a review on your favorite
bookseller website. Reviews are the best gift you give an author.

Titles you may like by P.S. Wells include:

**Quick Guides to Writing Well series**
*Pivotal Plots*
*Sensational Settings*
*Creative Characters*
*Dynamic Dialog*
*Point of View*

**Marc Wayne Adventure series**
*Chasing Sunrise*

Check out the audio version of *Chasing Sunrise* read by Scott Hoke

*The Patent*

*Secrecy Order*

*Unnatural Cause*

*Homeless for the Holidays*

Check out the audio version of *Homeless for the Holidays* read by voice actor Katie Leigh

## Personal Growth titles

*The Ten Best Decisions A Single Mom Can Make*

*Slavery in the Land of the Free*

*The Girl Who Wore Freedom*

C heck out these titles by PS Wells and PeggySue Wells

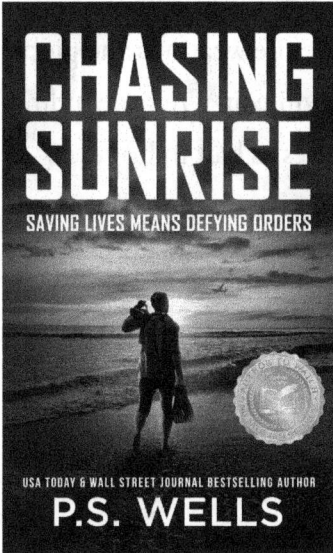

When an assignment results in a friend's death, Michael Northington seeks solace on St. Croix. When deadly players blow into St. Croix at the same time Hurricane Hugo unleashes its fury, will Michael's skills be enough to protect those he loves?

Also available in audio version, narrated by Scott Hoke.

When the world teeters on the verge of World War III, the nation that develops a patent attorney's invention will be militarily invincible in the race for global dominance. Now America's enemies have stolen the plans and kidnapped the inventor. Marc Wayne must find a way of escape before his captors realize the invention is theoretical. Or is it?

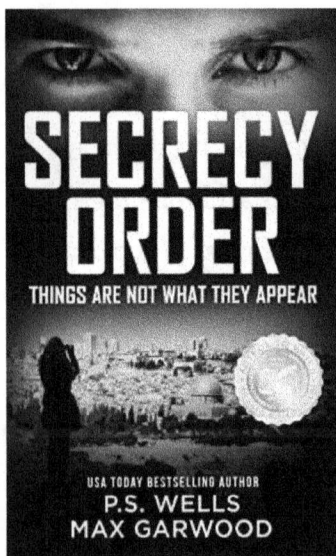

Powerful nations hunt for Marc Wayne and his invention which promises to redefine weapons and global warfare. Meanwhile, in a remote hiding place, Marc serves as bait in hopes to turn his predators into prey. When an illegal arms dealer leverages Marc for his own ends, will Marc ever see home and family again? As time runs out, can he trust the electro-physicist, Lei Quong, enough to escape with her?

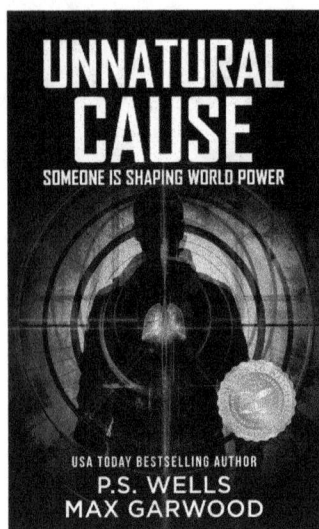

Winner of the best mystery suspense of the year, *Unnatural Cause* unpacks long unsolved family mysteries. Using a device that creates a deadly embolism from a remote location, someone is targeting world leaders to shape world power. But when Marc Wayne stops those who wield the ability to commit consequence-free murder, he finds he has played right into the mastermind's plans.

Christmas is coming, and Jack Baker's finances, friends, and future are as gone as last year's holiday. Amidst the holiday traditions and trappings, one family learns what is truly important when they lose all they have, and find they still have everything.

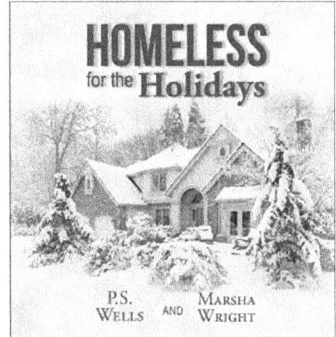

Also available in audio version read by voice actor Katie Leigh.

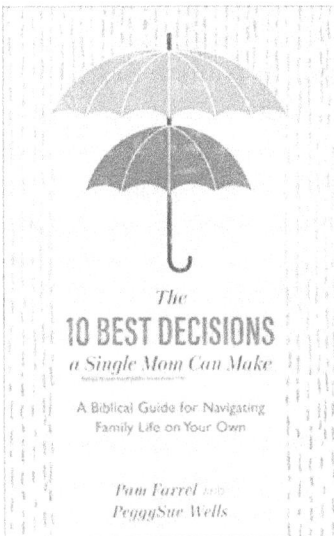

No matter how you became a single mom, you share the same challenges and fears all single moms have. How are you going to do this on your own? With humor, and sage advice, PeggySue Wells (single parent of seven children) provides practical helps and tangible tips to help you succeed.

A clear picture of how human trafficking happens and how prevalent it is today. We ended slavery once before in the United States, and we can do it again.

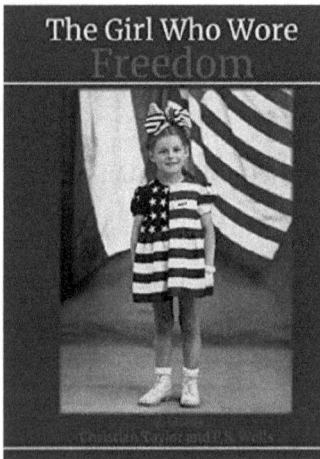

On June 6, 1944, when Dany was five years old, U.S. soldiers liberated her village from Nazi control. Soldiers established a base on Utah Beach near Dany's home, shared their provisions, and befriended the people of Sainte Marie du Mont. From the parachutes of the American soldiers who freed her, Dany's mother sewed a red, white, and blue dress resembling the American flag. Dany wore the dress at the yearly D-Day celebration and became known as *The Girl Who Wore Freedom*.

PeggySue's Particulars
to Pen

# POINT OF VIEW

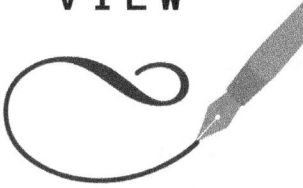

A Quick Guide to
Writing Well

PEGGYSUE WELLS

You want to write and write well. Point of view is the writer's most powerful tool to elicit emotion in the reader. POV can make the difference between a character appearing as a killer or a king. Learn how to pen the proper POV that compels a reader to turn pages until reaching the end.

You want to write and write well. Use this quick guide to amplify, intensify, and magnify through plot to craft a compelling story.

In this quick how-to guide, learn the particulars to craft pivotal plots that create compelling stories.

PeggySue's Particulars
to Pen

# PIVOTAL PLOTS

A Quick Guide To
Writing Well

PEGGYSUE WELLS

PeggySue's Particulars
to Pen

**CREATIVE
CHARACTERS**

A Quick Guide To
Writing Well

PEGGYSUE WELLS

You want to write and write well. Use this quick guide to craft creative characters that live in the reader's mind beyond the final page of a story.

Three essentials are common to every compelling story.

1) a character the reader cares about

2) a very great life-changing, world-impacting need the character must achieve

3) a great obstacle between the character we care about and the character's life-changing, world-impacting need.

In Creative Characters, learn how to craft characters who are believable, three-dimensional, and remain in the reader's memory long after the book is read.

Stories happen in a place and that place is the setting. Settings come in four personalities.

The personalities types of setting are

- Passive

- Active

- Like a Character

- Is the Story

PeggySue's Particulars to Pen

# SENSATIONAL SETTINGS

A Quick Guide To Writing Well

PEGGYSUE WELLS

What does the setting sound like, feel like, and look like? If you plan to write a book or want to improve a story, place the tale in a sensational setting. Sensational Settings: A Quick Guide to Writing Well shows you how.

PeggySue's Particulars
to Pen

**DYNAMIC
DIALOG**

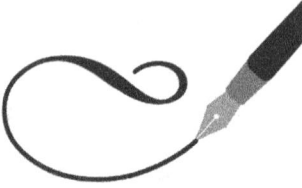

A Quick Guide To
Writing Well

PEGGYSUE WELLS

Dialog is what characters say. Powerful stories are dialog-driven through carefully chosen word selections. The four purposes of dialog in your story include:

1. Move your story forward

2. Reveal something important about your plot

3. Show something important about your character

4. Give your character a unique voice

Conversations that take place between characters are often the reader's favorite part. Add value to your story by writing dialog that is clever, creative, and concise.

# About the Author

P.S. Wells is a USA Today and Wall Street Journal bestselling author of 40 books (so far). When not writing, Wells rides horses, parasails, scuba dives, and skydives. She is the founder of SingleMomCircle.com

Connect with P.S. Wells at PeggySueWells.com

www.ingramcontent.com/pod-product-compliance
Lightning Source LLC
Chambersburg PA
CBHW060530280326
41933CB00014B/3122